MICHAEL JORDAN

NICK EDWARDS

SCHOLASTIC INC.
New York Toronto London Auckland Sydney

For Uncle Donald,
my sports buddy

PHOTO CREDITS

Front cover: © Barry Gossage/NBA photos.
Back cover: © Brian Drake/Sports Chrome East/West.
Interiors:
Pp. 1, 5, 16, 31: © Duomo/William R. Sallaz.
Pp. 3, 9, 10, 11: © Focus On Sports.
P. 4: © Noren Trotman/NBA photos.
P. 6: © The Sports Gallery.
P. 7: © Michael J. Okoniewski/Gamma Liason.
Pp. 8, 19, 32: © Andrew D. Bernstein/NBA photos.
Pp. 12, 13, 14, 15: © Jerry Watcher/Focus On Sports.
Pp. 17, 18, 29(r): © Nathaniel S. Butler/NBA photos.
P. 20: © ALLSPORT USA/Mike Powell.
P. 21: © Vincent Laforet/Gamma Liason.
P. 22(l): © Michael Springer/Gamma Liason.
Pp. 22(r), 23: © Bill Swersey/Gamma Liason.
P. 25: ©AP/Wide World Photos.
P. 27: © Walter Iooss, Jr./Sports Illustrated.
P .28: © ALLSPORT USA.
P. 29(l): © Scott Cunningham/NBA photos.

Photo researcher: Moya McAllister

ISBN 0-590-65173-0

12 11 10 9 8 7 6 5 4 3 2 1   5 6 7 8 9/9 0/0

Printed in the U.S.A.   24

First Scholastic printing, December 1995

Designed by Alfred Giuliani

Up in the air...it's a bird! It's a plane!
No, it's Michael "Air" Jordan!

Maybe Michael Jordan can't really fly, but it sure seems that way. He is also the best basketball player anyone has ever seen.

Michael grew up in Wilmington, North Carolina. He was born on February 17, 1963. He loved all sports, but basketball was his favorite. Michael spent hours playing in his backyard with his big brother, Larry. Lots of times, Larry would beat him!

When Michael was in the tenth grade, he didn't even make his high school basketball team. After that, Michael started getting up at six in the morning every day to practice. His parents, James and Deloris, had taught him that drive and effort mattered more than talent. So, Michael worked very hard.

Michael comes from a close family. As a little boy, Michael always saw his father stick out his tongue when he was concentrating. He admired his father so much that he started sticking out his tongue, too! Even today, that is a habit Michael has never broken.

By the time he graduated from high school, Michael was such a good basketball player that he could have gone to lots of different colleges. He chose the University of North Carolina, because it was his mother's favorite school.

During his freshman year, he led his team to the 1982 NCAA Finals. It was the first time that the Tar Heels had won a national championship in twenty-five years. In the last game, Michael even scored the game-winning basket.

Michael also played in the 1984 Olympic Games. He
helped the United States basketball team win a gold medal!

In the 1984 NBA draft, Michael was the third player selected. It is hard to believe that he wasn't picked first. The two teams that decided not to choose the skinny, young guard must feel very silly now.

When Michael joined the Chicago Bulls, he became a star right away. He scored sixteen points in his first official game, and never looked back. The Bulls even made the play-offs for the first time in years. Michael was so good that he was picked to play in the NBA All-Star Game, too.

At the end of that season, Michael won the Rookie of the Year Award. No one had ever seen a player who could jump so high and stay in the air so long! With a basketball in his hand, Michael was like a magician.

There are lots of great players in the NBA, but Michael was very special. During every game, he would do something new and exciting. No matter how many people tried to guard him, Michael could still find a way to score. Michael made shots no one else had ever tried before. Sometimes, he would even change his mind in midair and try another kind of shot.

But Michael wanted to do more than just slam-dunk the ball and shoot baskets. Every day during practice, he would play harder than anyone else on the team. Michael knew how important it was to be a complete and well-rounded player, and all that effort paid off. Michael helped the Bulls win three NBA championships in a row!

In 1992, Michael played for the Olympic Dream Team. His teammates were the biggest stars in the NBA, but Michael Jordan was the player everyone in the world wanted to see. No one was surprised when Michael helped the United States win yet another gold medal!

Then, in 1993, Michael decided that he had nothing left to prove as a basketball player. Even though he was only thirty years old, he decided to retire. Nine years is a short career for such a huge star, but Michael was ready to move on. It was time to try something new.

So Michael signed a minor league baseball contract with the Chicago White Sox. This was a very brave thing for him to do. Michael hadn't played baseball for almost fifteen years. But Michael liked to work hard, and he wasn't afraid to take risks.

Michael spent a full season in the minor leagues. Baseball is a very hard game to learn, and Michael had lots of ups and downs. But he also had fun. He even hit three home runs!

When Michael isn't playing professional sports, he likes to spend time with his wife Juanita and his three children. Their names are Jeffrey, Marcus, and Jasmine. Michael also enjoys listening to jazz and eating seafood pasta. He plays golf whenever he can, and he is very good. Someday, he may even try to become a pro golfer!

Michael really loves kids. He will often visit sick children in the hospital or appear at the Special Olympics. Michael's parents taught him that being a great player doesn't matter as much as being a good person.

In 1995, Michael realized how much he missed playing basketball. It was time to dust off his Nikes and go back to soaring through the air again! The Chicago Bulls were very excited to hear that their star was coming back.

After being away for so long, Michael wasn't sure how well he would play. But in only his fifth game back, Michael scored fifty-five points against the tough New York Knicks. He picked up right where he had left off!

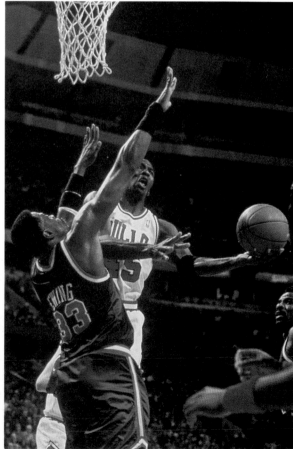

With Michael back in the NBA, basketball is a more exciting game than ever. Michael is eager to set new records and help the Bulls win more championships. But no matter how long he plays, watching Michael leap, and dive, and score is something his fans will never forget.